HOLIDAYS AND FESTIVALS

Diwali

Nancy Dickmann

Heinemann Library
Chicago, Illinois

www.heinemannraintree.com
Visit our website to find out
more information about
Heinemann-Raintree books.

To order:

☎ Phone 888-454-2279

💻 Visit www.heinemannraintree.com
to browse our catalog and order online.

Edited by Sian Smith, Nancy Dickmann, and Rebecca Rissman
Designed by Steve Mead
Picture research by Elizabeth Alexander
Production by Victoria Fitzgerald
Originated by Capstone Global Library Ltd
Printed and bound in China by South China Printing Company Ltd

The content consultant was Richard Aubrey. Richard is a teacher of Religious
Education with a particular interest in Philosophy for Children.

14 13 12 11 10
10 9 8 7 6 5 4 3 2 1

Library of Congress Cataloging-in-Publication Data
Dickmann, Nancy.
  Diwali / Nancy Dickmann.
     p. cm.—(Holidays and Festivals)
  Includes bibliographical references and index.
  ISBN 978-1-4329-4051-5 (hc)—ISBN 978-1-4329-4070-6 (pb)
1. Divali—Juvenile literature. I. Title.
  BL1239.82.D58D53 2011
  294.5'36—dc22   2010000081

Acknowledgments
We would like to thank the following for permission to reproduce
photographs: Alamy pp. **7** (© discpicture), **8** (© Tim Gainey), **9** (© Mary
Evans Picture Library), **16** (© Visage), **19**, **23 bottom** (© Peter Brown), **20**,
23 top (© Art Directors & TRIP), **21** (© Louise Batalla Duran); Corbis pp. **10**
(© Historical Picture Archive), **17** (© Mark Bryan Makela); Getty Images pp.
6, **23 bottom** (Narinder Nanu/AFP), **14** (Asif Hassan/AFP); Photolibrary
pp. **4** (India Picture), **5**, **23 top** (Mohammed Ansar/Imagestate), **11**, **12**,
15 (Photos India), **13** (Alex Mares-Manton/Asia Images); Shutterstock
pp. **18** (© jamalludin), **22 top left** (© Ronald Chung), **22 top right** (©
Nir Levy), **22 bottom left** (© Stephane Breton), **22 bottom right** (©
Mahantesh C Morabad).

Front cover photograph of traditional pooja thali reproduced with
permission of Photolibrary (Hemant Mehta/India Picture RF). Back cover
photograph reproduced with permission of Photolibrary (Photos India).

We would like to thank Diana Bentley, Dee Reid, Nancy Harris, and
Richard Aubrey for their invaluable help in the preparation of this book.

Every effort has been made to contact copyright holders of any material
reproduced in this book. Any omissions will be rectified in subsequent
printings if notice is given to the publisher.

Contents

What Is a Festival?

A festival is a time when people come together to celebrate.

Hindu people celebrate Diwali in the fall.

Sikh people also celebrate Diwali.

diva lamp

Diwali is called the Festival of Lights.
Special lamps are lit.

The Story of Diwali

Rama

Sita

Long ago, there was a prince called
Rama. He had a wife called Sita.

Sita was taken away by a wicked king. He was called Ravana.

Rama beat Ravana in a battle.
Sita was then able to come home.

People lit lamps to show Rama and Sita the way home.

Celebrating Diwali Today

At Diwali, some people think of the story of Rama and Sita.

Some people think of other stories about good beating evil.

diva lamp

People light lamps in their homes.

People draw pictures on their doorsteps.

People give cards and presents.

People dance and play music.

People watch fireworks.

mandir

People go to the mandir.

People welcome Lakshmi.

They hope she will bring good luck for the next year.

Look and See

diva lamp

fireworks

Lakshmi

pictures

Have you seen these things? They make people think of Diwali.

Picture glossary

Hindu people people who follow the teachings of the religion Hinduism

Lakshmi Hindu goddess of wealth and good fortune

mandir building where Hindus worship together

Sikh people people who believe in the teachings of the gurus. The gurus were important holy men in India.

Index

Note to Parents and Teachers

Before reading

Ask the children if they know what holidays and festivals are. Can they name any festivals they celebrate with their families? Discuss the difference between ordinary holidays and religious festivals. Explain that Diwali is a festival celebrated by Hindu people, who follow the religion of Hinduism and by Sikh people, who follow the religion of Sikhism. Diwali is sometimes spelled with a 'w' and sometimes spelled with a 'v' but both words refer to the same festival. Diwali is called the Festival of Lights.

After reading

• Read *Rama and the Demon King* by Jessica Souhami to the children. Explain that for many people Diwali is about the triumph of good over evil. Ask the children to think about the characters in the story. Which of them fit with the ideas of goodness or evil?

• Talk about diva lamps and things that light can stand for such as goodness, hope, and wisdom. Tell the children about other religions that use light as a symbol, such as the Jewish festival of Hanukkah. Show the children photos of divas and help them to design their own.

• Talk about Diwali as a time of optimism or hope and new beginnings. Discuss how this fits with traditional Diwali activities such as cleaning houses, sowing crops, or wearing new clothes. Ask the children to think of ways that they could make a 'new beginning'. You could suggest ideas such as sorting out differences with friends, starting a new project, or cleaning their room.